DISCOVERING

◆

ITALY

By Gordon Charleston

A ZOË BOOK

A ZOË BOOK

© 2000 Zoë Books Limited

Devised and produced by
Zoë Books Limited
15 Worthy Lane
Winchester
Hampshire SO23 7AB
England

First published in Great Britain in 2000 by
Zoë Books Limited
15 Worthy Lane
Winchester
Hampshire SO23 7AB

A record of the CIP data is available from the British Library.

ISBN 1 874488 90 8

Printed in Hong Kong by Midas Printing Ltd.
Design: Sterling Associates
Map: Sterling Associates
Production: Grahame Griffiths

Photographic acknowledgments
The publishers wish to acknowledge, with thanks, the following photographic sources:

Cover: Impact Photos/Louvet/Visa/Cedri; Title page Impact Photos/John Evans; 5l TRIP/TH-Foto Werbung; 5r Hutchison Picture Library/Julia Davey; 6 TRIP/TH-Foto Werbung; 7l TRIP/J Greenberg, 7r TRIP/F Bradbury; 8 TRIP/T Bognar; 9l Hutchison Picture Library; 9r TRIP/W Jacobs; 10 & 11l TRIP/T Bognar, 11r TRIP/BB Productions BV; 12 TRIP/T Bognar, 13t TRIP/N Bailey; 13b Impact Photos/Geray Sweeney; 14 TRIP/VB Schwanberg, 15l TRIP/T Yamashito, 15r TRIP/H Rogers; 16 TRIP/Phil Smith; 17t Hutchison Picture Library/Robert Aberman; 17b TRIP/J Moscrop; 18 Imogen Dawson; 19l TRIP/Eric Smith; 91r Hutchison Picture Library/J Davey; 20 Impact Photos/Alan Blair; 21l TRIP/A Tovy; 21r Impact Photos/Martin Black; Impact Photo/Mark Henley; 23l e.t.archive/Bibliotheque de l'Institute de Paris; 23r Redferns/Michel Linssen; 24 Hutchison Picture Library/John Hatt, 25l Hutchison Picture Library/Robert Francis; 25r Imogen Dawson; 26 Impact Photos/Ray Roberts; 27l e.t.archive/Museo Civico Modigliana, Italy, 27r e.t.archive; 28 TRIP/T Why, 29l TRIP/C Rennie; 29r Hutchison Picture Library/Trevor Page.

The publishers have made every effort to trace the copyright holders, but if they have inadvertently overlooked any, they will be pleased to make the necessary arrangement at the first opportunity.

Cover: *The leaning tower of Pisa*

Title page: *People dressed for the Carnival in Venice*

Contents

Italy

Area: 301 277 sq km
(116 324 sq miles)
Population: 57 650 000 (1998)
Capital: Rome

AUSTRIA

HUNGARY

The Dolomites

SWITZERLAND

SLOVENIA

The Alps

CROATIA

Mt Bianco
(4807m)

L Como

Trieste

Mt Cervino
(4478m)

L Maggiore

L Garda

Venice

FRANCE

Turin

Milan

Cremona

R Po

Pavia

BOSNIA

Parma

Genoa

Bologna

San Marino

Savona

Rimini

Florence

Ligurian Sea

Arezzo

Siena

Perugia

ITALY

Adriatic Sea

CORSICA

R Tiber

The Apennines

The Vatican City

Rome

Bari

Vesuvius

Naples

Pompeii

Brindisi

Amalfi

Taranto

SARDINIA

Tyrrhenian Sea

Stromboli

Ionian Sea

Mediterranean Sea

Reggio Calabria

N

Etna

Agrigento

SICILY

ALGERIA

TUNISIA

Syracuse

0   200 km

0   100 miles

Benvenuto!

Welcome to Italy. Italy is in southern Europe. It is shaped like a boot with a high heel. Next to the toe of the boot is the island of Sicily. Sicily and Sardinia are the largest of the islands around the coast that belong to Italy. There are two independent states within Italy. The tiny republic of San Marino is near Rimini and the Vatican City is an independent state within the city of Rome, Italy's capital city.

Italy is a mountainous country, with craggy, snow-laden mountains in the north and active volcanoes in the south. Only 20 per cent of the total area of the country is flat.

There are many differences between the north and the south of Italy. The south fits most people's ideas about Italy, with plenty of hot sunshine and very little rain. The central and northern regions are cooler and wetter

An ancient temple at Agrigento, Sicily

Window shopping in Milan

than the south. Most of Italy's industry is based in the north. The south of Italy is much poorer. The Italian government has tried to improve the south's industry and agriculture

Influence on the world

Italy is famous for its influence on art and culture. Some of the world's greatest artists, scientists and writers have come from Italy. The ancient Romans built up an empire that changed the course of European history and culture.

One country

Today Italy is one nation, but after the Roman empire ended, the country was invaded by foreign armies. Different regions became separate independent states. Italy did not become a single, fully united country until 1870.

Mountains and lakes

The Dolomite mountains in South Tyrol

Italy has two important mountain ranges, the Alps and the Apennines. The Alps stretch across the northern part of the country, and include some of the tallest mountains in Europe. Monte Bianco (also known as Mont Blanc) is on Italy's border with France and towers to 4807 metres (15 771 feet). Monte Cervino (also known as the Matterhorn) is on the border with Switzerland and reaches 4478 metres (14 691 feet). These are two of the best-known mountains in the Alps and attract climbers all year round.

In the eastern part of the Alps are the Dolomite mountains which are made of dolomite stone, a kind of hard chalk. These mountains have been shaped by wind, rain and ice into jagged peaks and deep gorges. Large numbers of tourists come to enjoy the beautiful scenery and to ski in the Dolomites.

A backbone of mountains

The other mountain range is the Apennines. This range gives Italy a kind of backbone. Its mountains spread in a line from the Alps in the north right down to the island of Sicily. In the northern Apennines there are quarries from which world-famous

Stromboli, an island volcano

marble is cut. This type of stone has been used for centuries to make magnificent buildings and statues.

Eruption!

Italy has three active volcanoes in the south - Etna, Stromboli and Vesuvius. Italy's most famous volcano is Vesuvius, which overlooks Naples. Vesuvius erupted violently in AD79, burying the ancient city of Pompeii in ash and lava. This preserved the city exactly as it was when the volcano erupted. Today people from all over the world come to visit Pompeii to see how the ancient Romans lived. Vesuvius hasn't erupted since 1944, but Etna and Stromboli are among the most active volcanoes in the world. Central and southern Italy are also shaken by earthquakes and some have been severe. In 1980 an earthquake in the area near Naples killed more than 1000 people.

The Lakes

Italy has many lakes, but the most famous ones are in the Alps. Holidaymakers from all over the world come to the lakes here, such as Como, Maggiore and Garda. The area is also popular with Italians, especially those who like windsurfing and sailing.

Brenzone, Lake Garda

National Parks

There are several National Parks in Italy, mainly in the mountains. There are also many State Nature Reserves and Regional Parks all over the country. Here the wildlife and habitats are protected. They help to to preserve wildlife such as bears, deer, eagles and flamingos. The Parks are also popular with walkers and hikers.

By the sea

Fishing boats at Syracuse in Sicily. The ancient Greeks built the first port here.

Since Italy is narrow and mostly surrounded by sea, it has a very long coastline - 10 000 kilometres (6000 miles). Many of its cities and towns are on or near the coast. Fishing boats work from the ports and harbours around the Italian coast. Some are still small family-owned boats, but these days most belong to large fleets.

Unfortunately the Mediterranean Sea is not well stocked with fish so the larger fleets go out to the Atlantic Ocean to catch fish.

Trading ports

Many of Italy's ports are used for trade. Italy does not have many natural resources, so raw materials such as petroleum have to be imported. The country also brings in meat and cereals. Italy's exports include manufactured goods, such as cars and machinery, ceramics, leather goods, food and wine. The main trading ports are Genoa, Trieste, Taranto, Venice, Savona and Naples.

Ferries sailing to Greece and other neighbouring countries leave from ports such as Bari and Brindisi.

Beaches and pollution

With such a long coastline, Italy has many beaches to attract holidaymakers. Despite efforts by the European Union and the Italian government to clean up the seas and beaches around Italy,

The busy port of Genoa

many areas are still polluted. The cleanest beaches are to be found on the large island of Sardinia. Many Italians spend their summer holidays there.

Sardinia

According to legend, when God finished making the world, he had some earth left over which he threw into the Mediterranean Sea. Then he stepped on this earth to create the island of Sardinia. It is the second largest island in the Mediterranean, after Sicily.

The Sardinian people, the Sards, are different from those on the mainland of Italy. No one knows where the first Sards came from, but they have their own language, Sardo, which is more like ancient Latin than modern Italian.

Today, many people living on Sardinia make their living from tourism. The Sards also earn money from mining and from exporting food, wine, and cork to the mainland.

The Sardinian coastline

Venice

The famous city of Venice is built on islands in a shallow lagoon. The city has canals as its main thoroughfares instead of streets. People walk or travel by boat. Instead of buses, there are *vaporetto* or water buses.

Tourist love to ride on the gondolas, traditional boats rowed by a gondolier who stands at the back using a single oar.

Rome

The River Tiber runs through the centre of Rome.

Rome is Italy's capital city and one of the most famous cities in the world. It has been important since ancient times, when it was the centre of the Roman Empire. Rome has come to be known as 'The Eternal City' because of its long history.

Visitors

Many tourists come to Rome to visit its museums full of works of art, and to see the monuments and buildings which date back to ancient times.

Romulus and Remus

A legend says that Rome was founded by twins, Romulus and Remus, sons of Mars, the Roman god. They were abandoned as babies and saved by a she-wolf. To this day, the wolf is the symbol of the city.

The Colosseum, Rome

There is so much to see here that it would take a very long time to see it all. In fact, the Romans have a saying about this: 'For Rome, one life is not enough'.

Rome is an extremely popular place for shopping. Both tourists and the Italians themselves come here to buy the clothes, shoes and designer goods for which Italy is so famous.

Rushing traffic

On the streets of Rome, everyone is in a hurry. Cars, motorbikes and scooters rush past and pedestrians have to take real care. The fumes from the traffic cause air pollution which damages people's health and some of Rome's famous buildings and monuments.

The harmful chemicals in the polluted air eat away at the stone. Some of the monuments have been so badly affected that they are now wrapped in plastic to prevent them from crumbling away completely. The city authorities have brought in laws to reduce the number of cars going into the city, but the problem is still a serious one.

The Trevi Fountain in the centre of Rome

Where people live

Many Italians spend their summer holidays at the coast near Amalfi.

Italy has a population of more than 57 million people. A large proportion of them live in the north of the country in large industrial cities such as Milan and Turin. Some of these northern cities have now spread out so much that they almost join up with each other. Milan and the nearby cities of Cremona and Pavia form one of these mega-cities.

The population of the main cities, like Rome and Milan, almost doubles in size during the working week, as people pour in from surrounding towns to work in these cities.

Rural life

In the past most of Italy's land was used for farming and growing crops. The Italians call their country Italia. This is taken from a word in ancient Greek or Latin which means 'land of cattle'. Today only about 40 per cent of Italy's land is used for agriculture. Most of the farms are small.

Some have been modernized, but most of them, especially in the south and in the mountain areas are poor. Often, the farms have been in one family for generations. This is changing, however, as more and more young people leave their homes to look for work in the large cities of the north.

Language

The official language of Italy is Italian. Different versions, or dialects, of Italian are spoken in different parts of the country. These local dialects are often influenced by the language of another country. Italy has been invaded many times in its history. After the invaders left, local people still kept some of the words and sounds from the invaders' language.

The dialect spoken in the north of Italy has French, German or Slovene influences. The Italian spoken in

Italy has a good motorway network.

Venice sounds like Spanish or Portuguese. In the south and Sicily, the dialects can sound like Greek or Albanian. Some Arabic words are used by people in Sicily and Sardinia.

Official Italian, which everyone speaks as well as their local dialect, was based on the dialect of Florence. Official Italian is used on television, in newspapers and at school.

Turning the hay to dry in the sun

'Closed for the holidays'

Many Italians leave the city at the height of summer to escape the stifling heat. If you go to cities like Milan and Rome in August, you will find many shops and restaurants closed. The owners may put up a sign saying *Chiuso per ferie*, meaning 'closed for the holidays'. At this time the roads, trains and planes are full of Italians heading for the mountains or the coast.

Religion and festivals

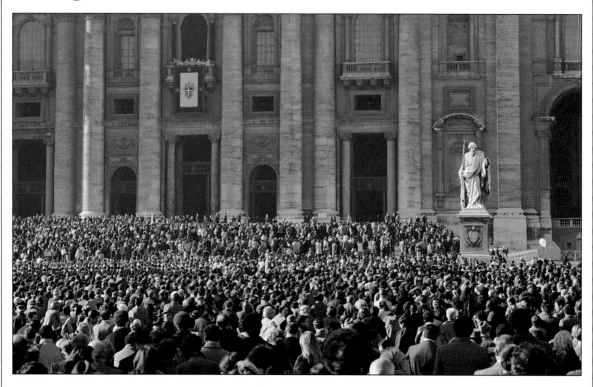

Most Italians belong to the Roman Catholic church. The Church and its traditions have a great influence on Italian society, even though fewer people go to church regularly now than in the past. Most children still take their first communion (known as confirmation) when they are about eight years old. This is an important ceremony in Italy. Children dress up in special white clothes for the occasion. In smaller cities and towns the children walk in a procession to the church.

The Vatican

Italy is the world centre of the Roman Catholic church. At the head of the church is the Pope, who lives in the

The Pope blesses the crowd in St.Peter's Square.

Vatican City. The Vatican City is an entirely separate state within the centre of Rome. The population is only about 1000 people, but the Vatican has its own government (the Roman Catholic church), its own car number plates, currency and postage stamps. It even

The Day of the Dead

There is a national holiday on 1 November to mark All Saints' Day. This is also known as the Day of the Dead. Families eat a formal meal, with an extra place set at the table in remembrance of relatives who have died. People also visit the graves of their relatives on this day.

Going to the carnival in Venice

has its own army, the Swiss Guards, who act as policemen in the city. They wear bright blue and orange uniforms.

The Vatican is full of things for tourists to see. There are churches and museums crammed with treasures from around the world. The Sistine Chapel is particularly famous, with its beautiful ceiling painted by Michelangelo. It took him four years to complete this work.

A chance to celebrate

Special religious events are often marked by holidays. Cities, towns and villages all have their local saint's day, when a statue of the saint is paraded through the streets. At Eastertime there are also processions in many places, with statues of Christ carried through the towns by people in white robes and hoods.

Early in the year, people celebrate *carnevale*. This is the last party before Lent, which is the time when Christians are supposed to give up luxuries until Easter. There are fancy dress parties and parades. The city of Venice has the most famous carnival and the city centre is closed off to make space for the parades.

Another famous festival is the Palio horse race which takes place in Siena every July and August. There is a parade of people in medieval costumes, with drumming and flag twirling, followed by a daring bareback horse race around the town square.

The Palio horse race in Siena

People at work

Grapes from vineyards between Florence and Siena are used to make a famous wine called Chianti.

Italy exports many food products but farming is not the most important part of the economy today. Since the 1950s Italy has built up her industries. These are particularly important in the north of the country, which has one of the most advanced industrial areas in Europe. Although this change has brought wealth it has also brought problems, such as pollution.

Manufacturing

Many Italian workers are employed in manufacturing goods. They produce many types of vehicles, and companies such as Fiat, Ferrari and Lancia are famous all over the world.

The Italians also manufacture electrical goods and machines. Italian companies export appliances such as washing machines and refrigerators to many foreign countries. Names like Indesit and Zanussi are known throughout Europe.

A sense of style

The Italians are known for their style. Their manufactured goods are often well designed. Milan in northern Italy is a world centre for fashion. Wealthy people all over the world wear clothes designed by the great fashion houses like Armani, Gucci, Valentino and Versace.

Canning tomatoes

Natural resources

Italy does not have many natural resources. Its most valuable is natural gas. There are also deposits of mercury, zinc and iron ore. Granite and marble are quarried in large amounts and Italian marble is world-famous.

An Italian racing car

Farming

The richest agricultural area in Italy is the Po Valley. This is the triangle of fertile plains in the northeast, around the River Po. The Po is Italy's longest river, at 653 kilometres (405 miles). It rises in the Alps and flows out into the Adriatic Sea.

Italy's most valuable crops are grapes and olives. Many people work to produce wine from the grapes and olive oil from the olives. Italy produces more wine than any other country in the world.

Grain crops such as wheat, corn and rice are grown on Italy's fertile plains, mainly in the north. The main fruit and vegetables grown in Italy are oranges, peaches, apples, persimmons, tomatoes and potatoes. More than half the world's artichokes come from Italy.

The main farm animals are cattle, pigs, chickens and sheep. Italians eat more meat than the farmers can produce, so Italy imports meat from other countries as well.

Everyday life

Many Italians start the day with a light breakfast, often no more than coffee or hot chocolate with a bread roll or a biscuit. Schools, shops and businesses open at 8 or 8.30am.

The day is usually arranged so that people take a long lunch break. In summer few people can work through the the intense heat during the middle of the day. The lunch break begins at 1pm and may go on until 3 or 4pm.

Lunch is the main meal of the day for many Italians and it includes a siesta or rest afterwards, out of the hot sun. This allows people to digest their food

In the centre of Rome many people take a walk, or passegiata, *to the Spanish Steps in the evening.*

properly. Businesses then re-open until around 7pm.

Dinner is often eaten at about 8pm, although in the hotter south people may eat later, at around 10pm. This is the time when the whole family can be together at the end of the day.

Walking and talking

The traditional *passegiata*, or promenade, is still a feature of life for many people. In the cool of the evening, before dinner, they join their neighbours in the local square or main street, to stroll and discuss the day's news.

Lunch served outside in Como

Family life

The family is very important to most Italians. In many places relatives live near one another, and children are often looked after by aunts, uncles or grandparents. Today, more young people from rural areas are leaving their family homes to go to the cities to find work.

Education

The school day starts early, but finishes at around 1.30pm. Children have homework to do every afternoon.

Children can go to nursery school from the age of three. From the age of six, all children have to go to Elementary School. They have to pass exams when they are 12, to go to Middle School until they are 14. If they fail, they stay at Elementary School until they pass the exams.

At present, students who pass their exams at Middle School, can choose to go on to a technical or art college or to go to a High School. Here they can take arts or science subjects, to prepare for university, or train to become accountants or teachers. Most courses at this level last for five years.

Students who pass their exams get a Diploma. Some then go on to university, where courses are free, for all who have a Diploma. However, there is so much demand for places, that universities select only those who have the best marks from their Diploma exams.

Sport

Many Italians are passionate about sport – both watching and playing. The most popular sport in Italy is *il calcio*, or soccer. There are many internationally famous clubs, like Juventus and AC Milan. Italy has also produced champions in cycling, skiing and basketball.

Playing football in the park

Buon appetito!

Most Italians prefer to dine together as a family. At weekends and in places where the family can get together in the middle of the day, lunch will be the main meal. It can last for hours as the family discusses the day's events.

The main meal of the day will usually start with *antipasto*. These are appetisers such as melon, olives, cold meats or salads. Next comes a pasta course or soup such as *minestrone*, made with pasta. This is followed by either a fish or meat course, with vegetables or a salad. Then there may be a selection of cheeses or fresh fruit. Homemade cakes and ice-cream are also popular desserts.

Shopping for cooked meats and cheeses at the market

Adults drink may drink wine or mineral water with the meal. Children usually have mineral water or fruit juice.

Coffee

After the meal, Italians love to drink coffee. There are many different ways to drink it. In the evenings the most popular are *espresso* and *macchiato*. *Espresso* coffee is very strong and is served without milk, in a very small cup. *Macchiato* has just a drop of milk added. *Cappuccino*, a bigger cup of frothy, milky coffee, is drunk in the morning.

Coffee at a café in Venice

Cooking styles

The different regions of Italy have their own special dishes and ways of cooking. The north is known for rich and creamy food. Many dishes are cooked with butter rather than olive oil. Here, people may eat dishes made with rice or polenta, which is made from maize, instead of pasta.

In the south flavours are often spicier and most dishes are cooked with oil rather than butter. Here fresh fish is often preferred to meat.

Parma ham

Parma, a town in northern Italy, is known for its high quality ham. It is made from the meat of pigs that have been fed on a special diet. The meat is rubbed with sugar, salt and spices, and then pressed and steamed. Finally it is rubbed with paper, before being stored for several months. This produces a fine, raw ham that is thinly sliced and served with figs or slices of melon.

Shopping for food

Panetteria - sells bread in all different shapes and sizes.
Pastificio - sells fresh pasta, in many different shapes, from *fusilli* (spirals) to *ravioli* (pasta cushions stuffed with spinach, herbs and meat).
Gelateria - sells ice-cream in many delicious flavours, such as *limone* (lemon), *cioccolato* (chocolate) and *nocciola* (hazelnut).
Salumeria - sells salami and other cooked meats, salads and cheeses.

Italian cheeses are world-famous. There are many different types. There is blue-veined gorgonzola, which has a strong taste, hard parmesan, which is often grated and sprinkled on top of pasta dishes, and soft, creamy mozzarella, which goes stringy when heated and is used to top pizza.

The ice-cream waiter

The arts

The centre of Florence dominated by the cathedral dome, designed by the great Renaissance architect, Brunelleschi.

The art for which Italy is most famous is the work created by sculptors and artists during the Renaissance. This was a time in the 14th and 15th centuries when there was a great blossoming in art, science and culture. People have called this time the Renaissance, or 'rebirth' because there seemed to be a rebirth of ideas and attitudes which changed the way that people thought. Many paintings and statues were made and magnificent buildings built, in new, exciting styles.

At that time, artists working in cities (particularly in Florence) were paid by wealthy families to produce great works for them. Three of the most famous Renaissance artists were Leonardo da Vinci, Michelangelo Buonarroti and Raphaele.

Leonardo da Vinci was both a scientist and an artist. He designed buildings, weapons and machines, as well as his paintings. He produced some of the most famous paintings in the world, including *The Last Supper* and *The Mona Lisa*.

Music

Italy is well-known for its rich musical heritage. It was Guido of Arezzo, an 11th century Italian monk, who first designed a way of writing down music. This method is still used today.

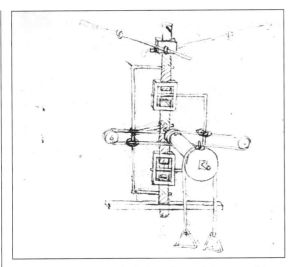

Leonardo Da Vinci's design for a flying machine

The finest violins ever made were produced in Cremona, near Milan, by a craftsman called Stradivari. It was also an Italian who invented the piano. Its full name, pianoforte, means 'soft-loud' in Italian. It was called this because it was the first keyboard instrument on which musicians could control the loudness of the music.

About 400 years ago, the Italians invented the type of musical theatre called opera. Italian composers such as Verdi and Puccini wrote many of the world's best-known operas, for example *Aida*, *La Traviata* and *Madame Butterfly*. The Italians also built magnificent theatres in which these operas could be performed. La Scala in Milan is one of the world's greatest opera houses.

Many great opera singers have come from Italy. Enrico Caruso was one of the 20th century's greatest tenors, and today Luciano Pavarotti is also world-famous.

Writing

In the world of literature and poetry, Italy has a rich past. Great writers from ancient Rome, like Ovid and Horace, are still studied today. The poets Dante Alighieri and Petrarch both lived in the 14th century. They became famous because they broke away from the usual writing styles of the time to try new approaches. Today writers such as Alberto Moravia, Natalia Ginsburg and Umberto Eco are world-famous.

Lights, camera, action

Italy is famous for its artistic films made by directors such as Visconti, Fellini and Bertolucci.

Today Italian films are world-famous and winning awards. *Mediterraneo*, directed by Gabriele Salvatores won an Oscar for best foreign film in 1992. *Life is Beautiful* won three Oscars in 1999, including one for Roberto Benigni as best actor.

Luciano Pavarotti

Ancient times

Ruins of the Forum, the centre of ancient Rome

There is evidence that groups of people lived in Italy during the Stone Age, more than 20 000 years ago. By the eighth century BC the ancient Greeks controlled much of the south of Italy and the island of Sicily. They built temples and cities such as Naples and Reggio Calabria.

No-one knows where the Etruscan people came from, but by 900BC they controlled much of north and central Italy. The Etruscans, like the Greeks, were traders and skilled craftspeople. Cities such as Bologna, Arezzo and Perugia were first built by them.

Rome takes over

According to legend, Rome was founded in 753BC. The Romans fought the neighbouring peoples and defeated them all, including the Etruscans. The Romans waited until they had control of the north of Italy before they attacked the Greek cities in the south. By 264BC the Romans had control of most of the country. They then set out to take over other countries around the Mediterranean.

The first conquests were in North Africa and Spain. The Romans went on to defeat all the surrounding countries and became the strongest power in Europe.

Consuls and emperors

At first the Romans were ruled by two consuls, who were elected. There was also a senate with representatives from the people. The idea was that all citizens would be equal. The reality was that while a few people became rich and powerful, the rest remained poor.

Huge numbers of slaves came to Rome from the conquered lands. The lives of these slaves depended on their masters. The wealthy masters used the slaves to build up large estates, pushing out poorer farmers. Around 73BC a gladiator called Spartacus led an uprising of 70 000 farmers and slaves against the leaders of Rome. The Roman army took two years to defeat them.

The way the Romans were ruled then changed. Instead of elected consuls, one strong ruler was appointed. He had complete control of the army and the government. Rome was then ruled by one dictator after another. In 27BC, the ruler Octavian took the title Augustus Caesar and became Rome's first emperor. For the next 500 years the rulers of the Roman Empire were called emperors.

During this time the Romans made great advances in architecture, engineering and the arts.

A house in the Roman city of Pompeii

A Roman bridge, rebuilt in the Middle Ages

The empire crumbles

By the third century AD, Rome had weak leaders. The empire had become so large, that it became more and more difficult to control it all. Tribes along the borders of the empire attacked the Romans. In AD476, the last Roman emperor, Romulus Augustulus, was overthrown and the empire ended.

Roman roads

The roads the Romans built in Italy and Europe are still to be seen today. These roads cross the countryside in long, straight lines. They helped the Romans keep control of their new territories. Troops and supplies could be moved quickly from one place to another.

Rulers and wars

For eight centuries following the fall of the Roman Empire, Italy was unsettled. Parts of the country were invaded by armies from France, Germany, Austria and Spain.

From the 11th century, several states based around cities such as Siena, became independent. As the foreign rulers became absorbed in problems back at home, the city states increased their power. By the 14th century the most important city states were Florence, Venice, Milan and Genoa.

Several of the cities came to be led by single families, such as the Visconti in Milan, and the Medici in Florence.

Spring *by Sandro Botticelli, a Renaissance painter supported by the Medici family in Florence*

These ruling families became very wealthy from trade. Many rich rulers spent a great deal of money to support architects, artists and scholars during the Renaissance.

The Renaissance ends

In 1527 Rome was attacked by Charles V of Spain. Times had become tougher, with economic hardship growing all over the country. This ended the golden age of the Renaissance.

Giuseppe Garibaldi

Over the next 270 years, Spain, Austria and France ruled different parts of Italy. Then Napoleon Bonaparte came to power in France. As part of his conquests he defeated all the other nations who held land in Italy. He took control of the country in 1798, but was defeated in 1815. Italy was divided again, with Austria taking the largest share of territory.

Moves to unite Italy

By now there was a strong feeling among the Italians against foreign rulers. A movement was started, which had the aim of uniting Italy under an Italian ruler. Giuseppe Garibaldi, was one of the movement's leaders. He formed an army known as the Redshirts. After some unsuccessful attempts, Garibaldi captured Sicily and most of the south of Italy. In 1861,

Victor Emmanuel II of Sardinia was proclaimed king of Italy. The last regions of Italy still had to be taken from Austria and France but finally, in 1870, the whole of Italy was united.

War and the Fascists

In 1915 Italy joined the First World War on the side of Britain and France. At the end of the war a new political party took power. This was the Fascist Party, lead by Benito Mussolini. He promised to restore order and put the country back on its feet. His real aim was to build up an empire like that of ancient Rome. Mussolini's troops used violence and fear to control the people.

In 1940, Mussolini took Italy into the Second World War on the side of the Germans. When the Allies invaded Sicily in 1943, Mussolini fell from power. Italy switched sides and fought against Germany for the rest of the war.

Benito Mussolini

Towards the future

The ceremonial Caribinieri *guards in Rome*

After the war ended in 1945, the Italians decided that they did not want a monarch to represent them as the head of the Italian state. The last king, Umberto II, stepped down. The Italians voted for a new Constitution, which came into effect in 1948. Italy, like France, became a democratic republic with a President as head of state.

Italy has flourished since 1948. It joined the European Community (EC) when it started in 1957. Since then Italy has increased its trade with its European partners, particularly France and Germany. The Italian economy grew stronger through the 1950s and 1960s, with some help from American aid, but also with a lot of hard work. There was another period of growth in the 1980s, which made Italy one of the world's leading economic powers.

Changing governments

Italy has many problems too. The Italians find it difficult to elect a settled government. There have been more than 50 different governments since 1948. It has been difficult to control the amount that the government spends on services such as pensions, health and education. The government

Palazzo Montecitorio, the lower House of Parliament, in Rome

has been struggling to reduce the amount that Italy borrows. It needed to do this so that Italy could join the single European currency in 1999. Many Italians have protested about the cuts in public services.

Many people in the richer, more industrialized north now resent the fact that their taxes are paying for costly projects in the poorer areas of the south. The Northern League is a political party which, among other things, is trying to stop this movement of money from the north to the south.

Jobs and crime

In recent years the number of people who cannot find jobs has increased. People from poorer countries in Africa and Eastern Europe have also come to Italy to work illegally. There have been an increasing number of racial attacks.

The government also has a problem trying to deal with organized crime. The Mafia is just one of three illegal, secret organizations which operate in Italy. They deal in drugs, gun-running and other criminal activities and have a great influence on Italian society.

Italy today

The Italian economy is now one of the largest in the world, after the USA, Japan, Germany and France. Italy is a leading member of the European Union (EU). The Italian people are proud of their country's achievements and of their history and culture.

A protest against racism

Fact file

Government

Italy is a democratic country, which means that the people elect the rulers. There is no king or queen. This kind of country is called a republic. The leader of the country is the President. Members of Parliament elect the President for a seven year term. The president appoints the Prime Minister, who is the head of the government.

The Italian Parliament is divided into two houses, the Chamber of Deputies has 630 members and the Senate has 315 members. Members of Parliament are elected by the people for a five year term. Voters must be over 18 years of age and Italian citizens.

There are many political parties in Italy. Parties that share some of the same aims group together in alliances to try to get a majority in Parliament.

Flag

Italy's red, white and green flag is called *La Bandiera*. It was used for the first time in 1796 by students in Bologna, who were fighting for independence. The colours were chosen so that the flag looked like the French republic's three coloured flag. Green, the colour of hope, was chosen instead of the blue on the French flag.

National anthem

The Italian national anthem is *Fratelli d'Italia*, which means 'Brothers of Italy'.

Religion

Italy has no official religion, but most Italians are Roman Catholic. There are also some Protestants and Jews and Muslims living in Italy, as well as people who do not follow any religion.

Money

The unit of currency in Italy is the lira (the plural is lire). In 2002 Euro notes and coins will be issued as common currency.

Education

There are both private and state schools in Italy. Private schools are mostly run by the Church.

Education is compulsory from the age of six to 14 years. There are plans to raise the school leaving age and to change the education system.

Newspapers and television

Two of the best-selling national newspapers are *La Repubblica* and *Corriere della Sera*. There are also many regional newspapers and weekly magazines.

On television there are three state-owned channels and three commercial channels. There are also satellite and cable television channels.

There are also three state-owned radio stations and many popular commercial radio stations.

Some famous people

Julius Caesar (100-44BC) was a Roman general and statesman

Dante Alighieri (1265-1321) was a poet

Giovanni Boccaccio (1313-75) was one of the earliest great writers of prose

Christopher Columbus (1451-1506) was an explorer

Leonardo da Vinci (1452-1519) was a leading figure of the Renaissance

Niccolo Machiavelli (1469-1527) was a political adviser and writer

Michelangelo Buonarroti (1475-1564) was a sculptor, poet and painter

Caterina de' Medici (1519-89) was a member of the important Medici family of Florence, who became queen of France

Niccolo Paganini (1782-1840) was a famous violin player

Giuseppe Mazzini (1805-72) was a writer and political thinker

Giuseppe Garibaldi (1807-82) was a soldier

Camillo di Cavour (1810-61) was a politician and diplomat

Giuseppe Verdi (1813-1901) composed many operas

Guglielmo Marconi (1874-1937) pioneered radio

Benito Mussolini (1883-1945) became leader of Italy in 1922

Natalia Ginzburg (1916-93) was a world famous novelist

Federico Fellini (1920-93) was a famous film director

Some key events in history

1000-800 BC The ancient Greeks established control of southern Italy

900 BC Etruscans arrived in Italy

753 BC Rome was founded

AD 96-180 The Roman Empire reached its peak of power

476 The last Roman emperor, Romulus Augustulus, was overthrown

c1300 The Renaissance began in Italy

1527 Rome was taken by Charles V of Spain

1798 Napoleon Bonaparte seized Italy

1815 Italy was returned to its former rulers after the defeat of Napoleon

1861 Kingdom of Italy formed

1870 Rome became part of Italy, finally uniting the country

1915 Italy joined the First World War

1922 Benito Mussolini came to power

1940 Italy joined the Second World War

1943 Italy surrendered to the Allies

1946 Italians voted to change from a Monarchy to a Republic

1957 Italy became a founding member of the European Community (EC)

1978 Former Prime Minister Aldo Moro was murdered by terrorists

1982 The Italian government passed the first ever anti-Mafia law

1992 Giovanni Falconi, a magistrate who lead prosecutions against the Mafia was killed by them

1992 A group of magistrates in Milan start action against politicians taking bribes and the businesses who gave them out to get government contracts

1999 Italy adopts the Euro as currency

Index